IT'S SO COLD IN MINNESOTA...™

BY BONNIE STEWART
AND CATHY McGLYNN

BLUE SKY MARKETING INC.
PO Box 21583-S St. Paul, MN 55121 USA

It's So Cold In Minnesota...™
Copyright© — 1997 by Bonnie Stewart and Cathy McGlynn
Design by Scott Drude
Printed in the United States of America
ISBN: 0-911493-18-2

Published by:
BLUE SKY MARKETING INC.
PO Box 21583-S
St. Paul, MN 55121 USA
(612) 456-5602
SAN 263-9394

8   7   6   5

DEDICATED TO:

Our fellow, hearty Minnesotans, who bravely faced the elements during the record-breaking cold winter of '96...and to our families and friends who so willingly gave us their answers to the statement, "It's So Cold In Minnesota...". You, along with the weather, were indeed our inspiration!

IT'S SO COLD IN MINNESOTA...

WHEN YOU INHALE,
YOUR NOSTRILS STICK TOGETHER!

IT'S SO COLD IN MINNESOTA...

PEOPLE USE TWO SETS OF KEYS
SO THEY DON'T HAVE TO TURN OFF THE CAR
WHILE SHOPPING

IT'S SO COLD IN MINNESOTA...

A 'CONGA LINE' REFERS TO A FORMATION OF SNOW PLOWS, NOT A LATIN DANCE

IT'S SO COLD IN MINNESOTA...

WHEN YOU COME IN FROM OUTSIDE, YOUR GLASSES FOG UP SO BAD YOU CAN'T SEE!

IT'S SO COLD
IN MINNESOTA...

SEVERAL PEOPLE DROWN EVERY YEAR ATTEMPTING
TO DIG BASEMENTS FOR THEIR
ICE FISHING HOUSES

IT'S SO COLD IN MINNESOTA...

WHEN YOU BLOW BUBBLES, THEY FREEZE AND YOU CAN PICK THEM UP

IT'S SO COLD IN MINNESOTA...

KNOBS ON CAR RADIOS DON'T TURN BECAUSE THEY'RE FROZEN

IT'S SO COLD IN MINNESOTA...

PEOPLE CAN'T TELL IF YOUR SPEECH IS SLURRED
FROM DRINKING OR BECAUSE YOUR FACE
IS NUMB

IT'S SO COLD IN MINNESOTA...

YOU THINK YOU KICKED A ROCK ON THE SIDEWALK AND THEN REALIZE IT'S DOG-DOO!

IT'S SO COLD IN MINNESOTA...

YOU DON'T HAVE TO BE JESUS
TO WALK ON WATER

IN 1996 THE MUNICIPAL SNOW DUMP IN
DULUTH DIDN'T MELT UNTIL JULY 20
(THE NEW RECORD!)

IT'S SO COLD
IN MINNESOTA...

THAT PEOPLE DON'T LOOK TWICE IF A MAN
WALKS INTO A BANK WEARING A SKI MASK

IT'S SO COLD
IN MINNESOTA...

YOUR DOORS FREEZE AND YOU CAN'T
GET IN YOUR CAR

IT'S SO COLD IN MINNESOTA...

YOUR DOORS FREEZE AND YOU CAN'T GET <u>OUT</u> OF YOUR CAR

IT'S SO COLD IN MINNESOTA...

MEN WALK AROUND WITH ICICLES HANGING FROM THEIR BEARDS

IT'S SO COLD IN MINNESOTA...

CHILDREN WEAR SO MANY LAYERS OF CLOTHING
THAT THEY CAN'T GET UP IF THEY FALL DOWN

IT'S SO COLD
IN MINNESOTA...

YOUR CAR FINALLY STARTS BLOWING WARM AIR
JUST AS YOU PULL INTO
THE PARKING LOT AT WORK

IT'S SO COLD IN MINNESOTA...

THERE ARE 'BLACK ICE' WARNINGS
(WHEN THE MOISTURE FROM CAR EXHAUST FREEZES ON THE PAVEMENT)

THE #1 EXCUSE FOR NOT GOING TO WORK IS
"IT'S TOO DARN COLD!"

THE #2 EXCUSE FOR NOT GOING TO WORK IS
"I FORGOT TO PLUG IN MY CAR"

IT'S SO COLD
IN MINNESOTA...

WHEN YOU SEE THE MORNING TEMPERATURE
IS -28° F YOU'RE HAPPY, BECAUSE IT'S GOING TO BE
A NICE DAY!

IT'S SO COLD IN MINNESOTA...

FROSTY THE SNOWMAN ASKS TO COME IN THE HOUSE!

IT'S SO COLD IN MINNESOTA...

YOU CAN POUND NAILS WITH A FROZEN BANANA!

IT'S SO COLD IN MINNESOTA...

INSTRUCTORS CONSIDER HOLDING SPRING
CANOE LESSONS IN INDOOR SWIMMING POOLS

IT'S SO COLD IN MINNESOTA...

WE HAVE NINE MONTHS OF WINTER AND
THREE MONTHS OF TOUGH SLEDDING

IT'S SO COLD IN MINNESOTA...

IT KEEPS THE RIFF RAFF OUT

IT'S SO COLD
IN MINNESOTA...

THE BIGGEST ACCOMPLISHMENT OF THE DAY IS
GETTING YOUR CAR STARTED!

IT'S SO COLD
IN MINNESOTA...

RADIO STATIONS AND BARS HOLD CONTESTS TO
SEE WHO CAN BEST IMITATE THE SOUND OF A CAR
TRYING TO START

IT'S SO COLD IN MINNESOTA...

THAT FOR FUN, WE THROW CUPS OF HOT WATER
OUT OUR BACK DOORS TO WATCH IT CRYSTALLIZE
IN MIDAIR

IT'S SO COLD
IN MINNESOTA...

PEOPLE MOVE TO ALASKA BECAUSE
IT'S WARMER!

IT'S SO COLD IN MINNESOTA...

THEY SOMETIMES HAVE TO CANCEL WINTER
SURVIVAL CLASSES!

IT'S SO COLD IN MINNESOTA...

PEOPLE MIGRATE SOUTH FOR THE WINTER JUST LIKE MANY BIRDS

(WE EVEN HAVE A NAME FOR THEM - 'SNOWBIRDS')

IT'S SO COLD IN MINNESOTA...

ABANDONED OR SNOWED IN CARS ARE NICKNAMED 'SNOWBIRDS' (ALTERNATE DEFINITION)

IT'S SO COLD
IN MINNESOTA...

THE #1 GREETING IS "COLD ENOUGH FOR YA?"

IT'S SO COLD IN MINNESOTA...

THE #2 SAYING IS "I CAN'T WAIT UNTIL THOSE DARN
MOSQUITOES GET HERE, AT LEAST IT'LL BE WARM!"

(IN SUMMER, THE #2 SAYING IS "I CAN'T WAIT UNTIL WINTER,
AT LEAST THERE WON'T BE ANY DARN MOSQUITOES!")

IT'S SO COLD IN MINNESOTA...

THEY CANCEL SCHOOL AND EVEN FUNERALS!
(THE GOVERNOR MAY EVEN CANCEL SCHOOL IN THE <u>ENTIRE</u> STATE!)

IT'S SO COLD IN MINNESOTA...

WE SOMETIMES HAVE TO CALL OUR NEIGHBORS TO SHOVEL THE SNOW AWAY FROM THE DOOR SO WE CAN GET <u>OUT</u> OF THE HOUSE!

IT'S SO COLD
IN MINNESOTA...

THE #1 RESPONSE TO "HOW ARE YOU?" IS "COLD!"

IT'S SO COLD IN MINNESOTA...

WHEN YOU SIT ON A TOILET, THE SEAT IS SO COLD YOU DECIDE TO WAIT

IT'S SO COLD
IN MINNESOTA...

INSTEAD OF SMOG WARNINGS, THERE ARE
WIND CHILL WARNINGS!

(SOME WARNINGS EXCEED 90° BELOW ZERO F)

IT'S SO COLD IN MINNESOTA...

WE SAW A STREAKER
AND HE WAS FROZEN IN PLACE!

IT'S SO COLD IN MINNESOTA...

WHEN YOU'RE ICE FISHING, YOU CAN HEAR THE FISH SHIVERING!

IT'S SO COLD
IN MINNESOTA...

PEOPLE WEAR LONG JOHNS UNDER
BUSINESS SUITS

IT'S SO COLD IN MINNESOTA...

MINNESOTANS SAY TO EACH OTHER,
"IT'S ⊚?✳! COLD OUT!" BUT TO A NON-MINNESOTAN
THEY'LL SAY "YUP, IT'S A LITTLE CHILLY TODAY"

IT'S SO COLD IN MINNESOTA...

IT'S A STATUS SYMBOL TO HAVE ARCTIC
EXPEDITION RATED BOOTS

IT'S SO COLD IN MINNESOTA...

WE 'GRILL' OUR CAR ENGINES WITH CHARCOAL BRIQUETTES TO WARM THEM UP!

IT'S SO COLD IN MINNESOTA...

DAILY ACTIVITIES ALWAYS "DEPEND ON THE WEATHER"

IT'S SO COLD IN MINNESOTA...

THAT PEOPLE USE HOCKEY STICKS
TO FIRE FROZEN DOG DOO INTO THEIR
NEIGHBORS' YARDS

IT'S SO COLD IN MINNESOTA...

HOUSES ACTUALLY CREAK, SNAP, AND POP
IN THE NIGHT

IT'S SO COLD IN MINNESOTA...

EVEN SENSUOUS WOMEN
WEAR WOOL SOCKS TO BED!

IT'S SO COLD IN MINNESOTA...

WHEN IT WARMS UP TO -10° F
YOU CAN UNZIP YOUR COAT

IT'S SO COLD IN MINNESOTA...

HOSPITALS REPORT
AN INCREASE IN BROKEN TOES, FROM PEOPLE
KICKING THE 'CHUNKS' OFF THEIR CARS

IT'S SO COLD IN MINNESOTA...

YOUR LONG JOHNS EVEN HAVE GOOSEBUMPS!

IT'S SO COLD IN MINNESOTA...

IT HURTS YOUR TEETH TO INHALE
THROUGH YOUR MOUTH

IT'S SO COLD IN MINNESOTA...

THAT ALL FLIGHTS LEAVING THE AIRPORT REFUSE TO COME BACK!

IT'S SO COLD IN MINNESOTA...

YOU CAN'T WAIT TO GET INTO AN ICE ARENA
TO WARM UP

IT'S SO COLD
IN MINNESOTA...

EVEN THE ALBERTA CLIPPERS SWING SOUTH
(THIS IS A TERM FOR A COLD FRONT, NOT A GROUP OF BARBERS)

IT'S SO COLD
IN MINNESOTA...

YOU GET OUT OF THE CAR TO CHECK THE
TIRES... NOT BECAUSE YOU THINK THEY'RE FLAT,
BUT BECAUSE YOU THINK THEY'RE SQUARE!

IT'S SO COLD
IN MINNESOTA...

YOUR FIRST BREATH UPON GOING OUTSIDE IS
MORE LIKE A GASP!

IT'S SO COLD IN MINNESOTA...

9 MONTHS AFTER A COLD SNAP OR BLIZZARD,
THE HOSPITALS ARE FULL OF NEW BABIES!

IT'S SO COLD IN MINNESOTA...

RUDOLPH'S NOSE GETS SO COLD IT TURNS BLUE!

IT'S SO COLD IN MINNESOTA...

THAT TOWNS COMPETE
TO SEE WHICH IS COLDER!
(THE CITY OF TOWER HOLDS THE RECORD OF -60° F SET IN 1996)

IT'S SO COLD
IN MINNESOTA...

WHEN IT'S 40°F <u>ABOVE</u> ZERO, PEOPLE START
WASHING THEIR CARS!

IT'S SO COLD IN MINNESOTA...

THERE ARE DOGS FROZEN TO FIRE HYDRANTS!

IT'S SO COLD
IN MINNESOTA...

THERE ARE MORE CARS THAT WON'T START
THAN CARS THAT WILL!

IT'S SO COLD IN MINNESOTA...

YOU HAVE ICE ON <u>BOTH</u> SIDES OF YOUR WINDSHIELD

IT'S SO COLD
IN MINNESOTA....

PEOPLE ARE TREATED FOR COLD BURNS RATHER
THAN SUNBURN!

IT'S SO COLD IN MINNESOTA...

THE #1 CHRISTMAS GIFT IS A CAR SURVIVAL KIT!

IT'S SO COLD
IN MINNESOTA...

THERE IS NOTHING ELSE TO TALK ABOUT

IT'S SO COLD IN MINNESOTA...

THAT THE CITY OF INTERNATIONAL FALLS, MN
WAS THE INSPIRATION FOR "FROSTBITE FALLS" IN
THE ROCKY AND BULLWINKLE CARTOONS

IT'S SO COLD IN MINNESOTA...

THE GROUNDHOG DOESN'T COME OUT UNTIL
MAY TO SEE IF THERE ARE 6 WEEKS LEFT
OF WINTER

IT'S SO COLD IN MINNESOTA...

THAT PEOPLE WEAR ELECTRIC SOCKS

IT'S SO COLD
IN MINNESOTA...

THAT MINNESOTANS WHO DON'T MIGRATE,
HIBERNATE

IT'S SO COLD
IN MINNESOTA...

YOU CAN COUNT ON AN INCREASE IN BEEF
PRICES BECAUSE BULLS GO STERILE (SOME REALLY DO!)

IT'S SO COLD IN MINNESOTA...

THERE ARE HEATED BUS SHELTERS ON CITY STREET CORNERS

IT'S SO COLD IN MINNESOTA...

SOME LAKE BOTTOMS DON'T THAW UNTIL THE MIDDLE OF JULY

(SOME SAY THE SAME THING ABOUT PEOPLE!)

IT'S SO COLD IN MINNESOTA...

LETTER CARRIERS LOOK LIKE THE
ABOMINABLE SNOWMAN

IT'S SO COLD IN MINNESOTA...

THE ST. PAUL WINTER CARNIVAL HOLDS
STOCK CAR RACES ON AREA <u>LAKES</u>!

IT'S SO COLD
IN MINNESOTA...

WE HAVE ONLY TWO SEASONS - "WINTER" AND
"ROAD REPAIR"

IT'S SO COLD IN MINNESOTA...

THE STATE HAS MORE MILES OF SNOWMOBILE
TRAILS THAN TRUNK HIGHWAYS (TRUE!)

IT'S SO COLD
IN MINNESOTA...

PEOPLE TOW REAL HOUSES ONTO LAKES SO
THEY CAN FISH IN COMFORT

(SOME HAVE TWO AND THREE BEDROOMS!)

IT'S SO COLD IN MINNESOTA...

THERE IS A THRIVING HOUSE RENTAL
BUSINESS - FOR ICE FISHING HOUSES!

IT'S SO COLD IN MINNESOTA...

DOWNTOWN MINNEAPOLIS AND ST. PAUL
COMBINED HAVE MORE THAN 10 MILES OF
'SKYWAYS'

(CLIMATE-CONTROLLED WALKWAYS) CONNECTING 92 BLOCKS!

IT'S SO COLD
IN MINNESOTA...

THAT THE "MINNESOTA HUNCH" IS THE NAME
FOR THE WAY WE WALK WITH OUR SHOULDERS
SCRUNCHED UP TO KEEP OUR NECKS WARM

IT'S SO COLD IN MINNESOTA...

THAT IN 1888, THE TALLEST BUILDING IN ST. PAUL
WAS MADE OF ICE!
(A 130 FOOT ICE CASTLE MADE WITH 55,000 BLOCKS OF ICE FOR THE ST. PAUL
WINTER CARNIVAL. IT WAS ALSO THE FIRST PUBLIC BUILDING
IN THE CITY TO USE ELECTRIC LIGHT!)

IT'S SO COLD
IN MINNESOTA...

THAT LAWYERS WILL SOMETIMES PUT THEIR
HANDS IN THEIR <u>OWN</u> POCKETS

IT'S SO COLD IN MINNESOTA...

THAT A BRASS BAND ON SNOW SHOES FURNISHED THE WEDDING MUSIC FOR A CEREMONY IN THE 1888 ST. PAUL WINTER CARNIVAL ICE PALACE

IT'S SO COLD
IN MINNESOTA...

YOUR GARAGE DOOR FREEZES SHUT AND YOU
CAN'T GET IN (OR OUT!)

IT'S SO COLD IN MINNESOTA...

PEOPLE IN CHICAGO SAY "IT'S COLD HERE,
BUT AT LEAST IT'S NOT MINNESOTA!"

IT'S SO COLD IN MINNESOTA...

THAT YOUR DOCTOR PUTS ON <u>YOUR</u> CLOTHES
AFTER YOU TAKE THEM OFF

OUR SINCERE THANKS TO THE FOLLOWING PEOPLE AND ORGANIZATIONS FOR THEIR CONTRIBUTIONS:

Bart Bender
Gene & Adelle Carr
Dave Carr
Dan Collins
Steve Foss
Bruce Hagovik

Caroline Hanrahan
Craig McKee
Don Peterson
Catherine Pringle
Karen Rienstra
Susan Schreifels
Kerri Spadaccini

Corinne Stefanson
Joe Stinchfield
Kathryn Ter Horst
Karen Vento
Kathy Winkler
KXJB-TV

St. Paul Festival & Heritage Foundation
St. Paul Department of Planning & Economic Development
Special thanks to the listeners of the Denny Long Show on WCCO radio

AFTERWORD...

As we laughed ourselves through this book project, we felt fortunate that we were able to have warm shelter and hot meals to sustain us through some of the coldest days that we have experienced. We know there were many families not as fortunate. In our sincerest respect to those who may have felt the cold more deeply than most, we are donating a portion of the profits of this book to "Loaves and Fishes," the Fosston, Minnesota food shelf, a local organization that assists many families in our area throughout the year.

Finally, if you'd like to send us your own additions to this book, we'd like to read them. We may even use them in our next edition! Please send them to us care of our publisher: Blue Sky Marketing, PO Box 21583, St. Paul, MN 55121 USA. Note that all items submitted become the property of the publisher and no compensation or recognition will be given.